EXTREME CAREERS

SMOKEJUMPERS

Life Fighting Fires

Mark Beyer

the rosen publishing group's
rosen central

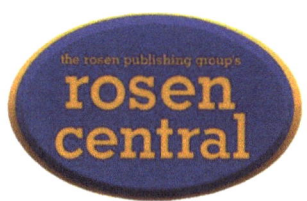

As always, to Lucy

Published in 2001 by The Rosen Publishing Group, Inc.
29 East 21st Street, New York, NY 10010

Copyright © 2001 by The Rosen Publishing Group, Inc.

First Edition

All rights reserved. No part of this book may be reproduced in any form without permission in writing from the publisher, except by a reviewer.

Library of Congress Cataloging-in-Publication Data

Beyer, Mark.
Smokejumpers: Life fighting fires / by Mark Beyer.—1st. ed.
p. cm. — (Extreme careers)
Includes bibliographical references (p.) and index.
ISBN 978-1-4358-8716-9
1. Smokejumpers—Juvenile literature. 2. Wildfire fighters—Juvenile literature. [1. Smokejumpers. 2. Wildfire fighters 3. Fire fighters.]
I. Title. II. Series:
SD421.23 .B.48 2001
634.9'618—cd21   00-010726

Manufactured in the United States of America

Contents

1 Extreme Risk — 4

2 Protecting Our Forests — 13

3 Smokejumper Training — 23

4 Jumping into a Fire — 33

5 Fighting Forest Fires — 43

Glossary — 56

For More Information — 58

For Further Reading — 61

Index — 62

Extreme Risk

Fighting forest wildfires is a dangerous business. Some wildfires, however, are easier to get to than others. They can begin to burn near roads, or they can move through low-lying forests, on flat ground or gentle slopes. These wildfires are fought bravely by ground crews of "hot shots." Hot shots can be a line of five, eighteen, or seventy men and women who are working very close to a blazing wall of fire.

Other wildfires burn in far off, remote areas of a forest. These wildfires can start in a deep gulch or high on a mountainside. These places are often far from roads. The only way to get to these blazes quickly is by dropping firefighters from planes. So what do you get when you cross a wildfire firefighter with a parachutist? That's right: a smokejumper.

When a wildfire occurs in a remote area, parachuting firefighters called smokejumpers are called in to battle the blaze.

Smokejumpers and hot shots are equally dedicated to putting out wildfires. Their mission is the same: stop wildfires before their destructive energy destroys the forest, kills the animals, or threatens human life. Smokejumpers have an added task, however. Before they even hit the ground, smokejumpers are hard at work tracking the fire, finding the right place to jump, and concentrating on landing safely.

Once on the ground, smokejumpers work the same way any forest firefighter does. They cut down trees

A firebreak is a wide dirt barrier created by firefighters to contain a forest fire.

and drag them from the wildfire's path. They dig up stumps. They chop away the underbrush. Then they turn the soil over and over until just dirt remains. All of this work is done while the fire creeps closer to them.

The firefighters create a firebreak, a wide dirt barrier, which is essential in helping to stop the spread of a wildfire. Sometimes, though, even fifty feet of dirt is not enough to keep sparks from drifting over to another dry forest area. Little sparks can create raging fires. Smokejumpers can work for days against a large wildfire. They might work eighteen

Extreme Risk

hours with only breaks for food. Their dedication has stopped the destruction of millions of acres of forests all over the world.

Daredevils with Higher Goals

Respect for smokejumpers was a long time coming. In the 1920s, forest firefighters suggested that parachuters be used to fight wildfires. Government officials rejected the idea. They said people who jumped out of airplanes were daredevils and thrill seekers, and such people could not be trusted to fight raging wildfires once they reached the ground.

Firefighters used to have to travel over difficult terrain to reach the site of a wildfire.

Smokejumpers: Life Fighting Fires

Such a policy forced hot shots to travel in jeeps, trucks, and sometimes on mules to reach remote areas to fight wildfires. These forested areas were on mountainsides, in deep gulches, or far beyond any roads. Getting to remote wildfires took hours of driving or days of hiking. Hot shots were exhausted by the time they reached the blaze. Oftentimes, when they finally reached the site, the wildfire had gotten much worse. To a great extent, all the hot shots' best efforts were wasted because so much forest destruction had already occurred.

By contrast, an airplane full of ten or twenty parachutists who knew firefighting could get to a remote area in minutes. They could drop down into a clearing near the fire. Their supplies and equipment could be dropped after them. Once gathered on the ground, parachuting firefighters could quickly get to a wildfire and put it out before it became larger or grew completely out of control.

By 1940, the idea of using parachutists to fight fires was finally put to the test. Parachutes and airplanes had become much more reliable and safe, and U.S. forestry officials wanted remote wildfires to be caught quickly, before they raged out of control.

Extreme Risk

The Nez Perce National Forest became the first place where a fire was fought beginning with a parachute drop. Soon, the U.S. Forest Service began training more smokejumpers.

Focus on Speed and Safety

Today's smokejumpers are highly trained, professional forest firefighters who understand the extreme danger of their job. Smokejumpers know that they must successfully manage speed with safety.

In the 1940s, the U.S. Forest Service began training smokejumpers.

Smokejumpers: Life Fighting Fires

How Wildfires Start

The U.S. Forest Service estimates that 125,000 forest fires occur each year in the United States, although most of these are quickly put out or controlled. Lightning starts many of these fires. There are millions of lightning strikes around the country each year. Lightning is super-heated electricity, and dry forest areas can easily ignite when lightning strikes. Humans, however, cause almost 90 percent of wildfires. Carelessly set campfires, lit matches, or burning cigarettes tossed on the ground are the most common causes of wildfires.

Smokejumper crews, called "sticks," not only must get to a fire quickly but also must get everyone to the ground, along with the necessary supplies and equipment. Only when they are safely on the ground are they able to focus on firefighting.

The Drop Zone

Sometimes, remote wildfires are small and only need two smokejumpers to snuff them out. Other fires become big quickly, and a stick of seventy-five or eighty smokejumpers must be sent into the forest. In any event, smokejumpers must find a drop zone where they can safely land. The pilot sits with a spotter in the cockpit. It is the spotter's job to look out the window and "spot" a good place for the smokejumpers to drop. The plane circles 200 feet above the trees. The spotter searches the terrain below. There is not always a clearing for smokejumpers to drop into. They sometimes have to drop down into the trees. When smokejumpers drop into trees, their parachutes almost always snag in the branches. Getting caught in the air like this during a wildfire is even more dangerous than being on the ground because there's nowhere to run.

Smokejumpers must quickly drop through the branches to the ground. They do this using a safety line called a ladder. Smokejumpers carry a ladder with them on every jump. Using a ladder is a lot like what mountain climbers do when they rappel down a cliff. As they hang in the trees, smokejumpers fasten the ladder onto their parachute harness. Then they release themselves from the harness and lower themselves slowly to the ground. Using a string ladder takes a lot of strength, which is one reason why all smokejumpers must be physically fit.

Smokejumpers: Life Fighting Fires

Why Take the Risk?

People might wonder why smokejumpers take such risks. During a wildfire, shifting winds can turn a small fire into an onrushing blaze. Smokejumpers put their lives at stake every time they jump from a plane into a fire. What makes people work under such dangerous, extreme conditions?

Protecting Our Forests 2

Smokejumpers and forest firefighters risk their lives to protect the forests. During a wildfire, animals and people are often put in danger. Getting to a fire and controlling its movement is important to everyone's safety. However, protecting people and saving animals from death are not the only reasons wildfires are fought. The importance of our forests as natural resources is one of the biggest reasons, too.

Animal Habitat

Animals are essential to human survival, and forests are where most birds and other animals live. Forests supply their food—providing plants, insects, nuts,

Animal populations are threatened by wildfires.

bark, berries, and other animals for them to eat. In turn, animals help to transfer the seeds of many plants from one area of the forest to another. They also control insect populations, and insects help to clean the animals' skin, fur, and feathers. When animals die, their bodies feed other animals and insects. Their rotting, decomposing bodies help plants grow. Plant and animal life interconnect; without one, you cannot have the other. Overall, animals help maintain the balance of nature.

Protecting Our Forests

You would think that animals would simply run away during a forest fire. Most do, but there are only so many places they can run to before an out-of-control fire catches up with them. Forest fires often create powerful winds that can reach speeds of over eighty miles per hour. That's as powerful as a hurricane. Caught in these wind drafts, birds cannot fly and are pushed back to the ground. Fire can easily kill birds caught by the wind drafts. Firefighters save the lives of many animals during every fire.

Wood Products

Lumber is not the only product we get from trees. Keeping forests safe from large, destructive fires benefits our daily lives in many ways. Tree sap is essential in many oils and tars. Varnishes used to coat wooden tables, desks, and chairs come from trees, and, of course, these tables, desks, and chairs come from trees, too. Some of the dyes used to color fabric can be traced back to trees. Important medicines, cooking herbs, and decorative bushes also come from forests. Finally, the paper on which you are reading these words is made from wood pulp, a substance formed from ground-up wood fiber. There are countless products that we all take for granted which are made from wood. If something is not made from metal, plastic, or soil, it probably has some wood in it. Without smokejumpers and hot shots working to put out raging fires, there would be fewer of all these products for us to buy, and the prices of these items would be much higher, too.

Trees, Brush, and Root Systems

Scientists have proven that the ground beneath the forest is as important as the trees themselves. This is because trees and other plants have root systems. Some roots are very thick, the size of your arm or leg. Other roots are smaller than the eye can see. All roots do one thing very well: They hold the ground together. When it rains, the roots soak up the water. As the water settles into the ground, it is channeled through the root systems. These systems have watersheds which are underground channels that supply creeks and

Root systems in the forest absorb rain and hold topsoil in place.

Smokejumpers: Life Fighting Fires

streams with water. In turn, these creeks, streams, rivers, and lakes supply the water that we use daily.

Without the root systems in place, rainwater would carry away the topsoil. When heavy rains carry a lot of soil and water downhill, floods and mudslides can occur. These natural forces have the strength to demolish hillsides and crush towns. Worse, once all the topsoil is eroded, we can no longer grow food to keep us alive.

Smokejumpers and forest firefighters are not just out for the thrill of fighting fires, and they are not on

When root systems are destroyed by fire, topsoil can be washed away by rain and floods and mudslides may occur.

Protecting Our Forests

the fire line simply to save the forest for campers and hikers. Smokejumpers work to protect and save forests for everyone's benefit.

Fire Detection

Fighting wildfires has improved over the years because people have developed better ways to spot fires before they rage out of control. Lookout towers, spotter planes, and weather satellites put people and electronic instruments in places where they can help.

Lookout Towers

Throughout U.S. forests, there are lookout towers, the most common vantage point from which to detect fires. Usually, they are built ten or twenty miles apart, and the tops of these towers rest just above the treetops, about ninety feet high. On top of the tower is a sort of cabin. Firewatchers are stationed in these cabins during wildfire season (May through September).

Every two or three weeks, a supply truck visits each tower to bring food, water, and supplies. Firewatchers patrol the forests by walking the

Firewatchers are stationed in lookout towers during wildfire season. They help locate fires and dispatch firefighters.

catwalk built around the outside of the cabin. They search the forests around them for smoke—a sure sign that a fire is burning. When a fire is detected, the firewatcher uses an azimuth indicator to determine its location. An azimuth indicator converts direction into a numerical compass reading. Once the direction has been determined, the firewatcher calls the fire control headquarters with the location of the fire. If the fire is in a remote area, the smokejumpers are called in.

Protecting Our Forests

Spotter Planes

Planes are an effective way to spot fires, too. They have the advantage of being mobile and can cover great distances quickly. Spotter planes detect forest fires using Fire Scan, a special infrared photography system. Unlike a regular camera, infrared photography can see through smoke. Fire Scan photography can pinpoint the exact location of the fire so that smokejumpers know where—and where not—to jump.

Computers and Weather Satellites

Computers help us do many things today, including forecast the weather. The U.S. Forest Service now uses weather forecasting to help

Spotter planes detect forest fires with a special infrared photography system called Fire Scan.

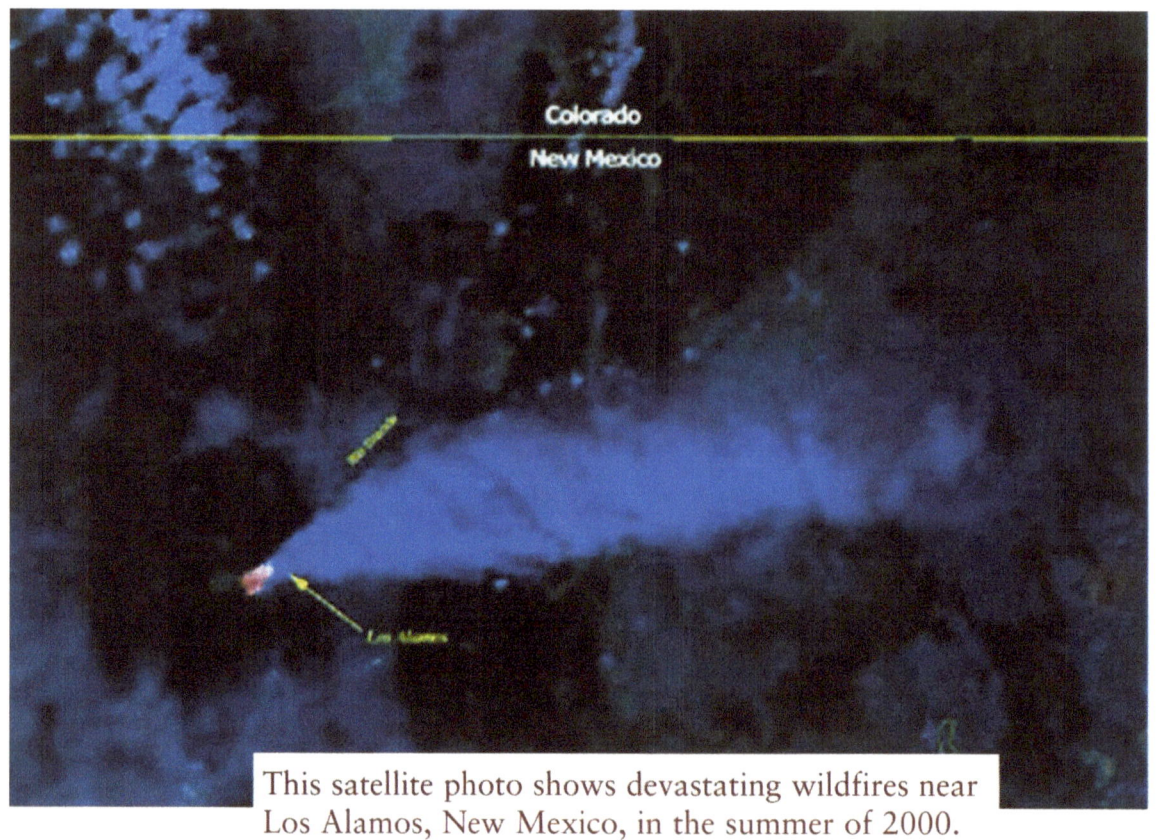

This satellite photo shows devastating wildfires near Los Alamos, New Mexico, in the summer of 2000.

determine when and where a wildfire is likely to occur. Wind direction, humidity (the amount of water in the air), and temperature can determine if a lightning strike will start a forest fire. With this knowledge, the forest service is able to alert its spotters to be on the lookout for fires during these dangerous weather conditions.

Smokejumper Training 3

If someone is not serious about fighting wildfires, smokejumping is not for him or her. In fact, only professional forest firefighters who have years of experience are recruited for smokejumping. Rookie smokejumpers have a minimum of four years of wildfire experience under their belts before they train to drop from airplanes into a remote blaze.

Strength and Endurance

As with all forest firefighting training, smokejumpers begin with physical training. Parachuting into dense areas or small clearings is difficult. Smokejumpers must have the strength to maneuver their parachutes.

The rigorous, four-week training program for smokejumpers is a lot like military boot camp.

When they land in a tree, they have to have the strength to release themselves from their parachute harness and climb down. When smokejumpers finally hit the ground and get to the fire, they need the strength to dig, cut, chop, and move dirt, brush, and timber away from the oncoming blaze. These jobs require strength, and they also require stamina; smokejumpers fight fires for many hours at a time. Smokejumpers often don't have the luxury of taking a break. Their lives depend on moving and working quickly, nonstop, for a whole day. The work of a smokejumper is physically and mentally grueling.

Training for Combat

This extreme career requires extreme training. Smokejumpers are waging war against a powerful enemy: fire. Therefore, smokejumpers must train as soldiers do. In fact, smokejumper training is a lot like military boot camp. The four-week training course combines physical, mental, and academic tests to see if recruits are up to the task of smokejumper firefighting.

There are weight, height, and other physical requirements that all smokejumpers must meet.

Smokejumpers: Life Fighting Fires

Blazing a Trail

In 1981, Deanne Shulman became the first female smokejumper. Since then, many more women have gone through training and become smokejumpers.

Smokejumpers must weigh between 120 and 200 pounds. Weight restrictions are a serious matter for smokejumpers. Someone weighing more than 200 pounds may not be able to safely maneuver and land a parachute. Weighing less than 120 pounds can be just as deadly for a smokejumper; the wind can blow the smokejumper off course. Imagine being blown into the middle of the blaze!

Smokejumpers must stand between five feet tall and six feet one inch tall. Their eyesight must be 20/20 with corrected lenses. A smokejumper's hearing is also tested. No smokejumper can

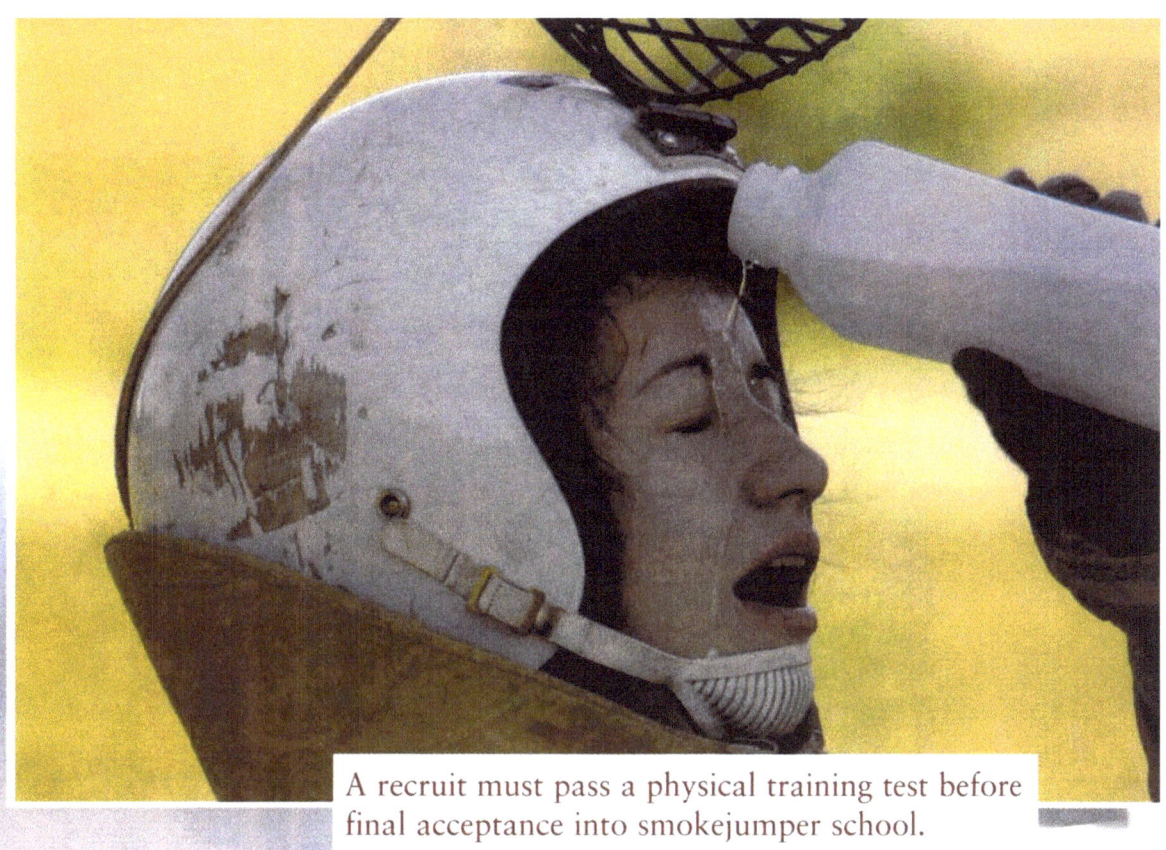

A recruit must pass a physical training test before final acceptance into smokejumper school.

have a loss of more than 25 decibels in each ear, meaning someone with a hearing aid cannot become a smokejumper.

Finally, each recruit must pass a physical training test before final acceptance into smokejumper school. The test is taken in a single session, with five-minute rest periods between exercises. A smokejumper must be able to do seven pull-ups, forty-five sit-ups, and twenty-five push-ups, and be able to run one and one-half miles in less than eleven minutes. You might think these requirements sound easy. Try them yourself. They are harder than you think. Also, these are minimum requirements. Out in the field fighting a wildfire, you can be sure the physical challenge will be more intense than doing the few sets of push-ups, sit-ups, and pull-ups that get you into the training program.

Wait, there's more. After the first week of training, all recruits must pass a "packout" test. This test requires recruits to carry a 110-pound pack of smokejumper equipment over a three-mile course in less than ninety minutes. Another packout test may be given later in the training.

Daily Training Routine

Not all training for smokejumpers is physical. After morning exercises and running, smokejumper trainees spend a lot of time in the classroom. Here they study firefighting techniques. They learn how wildfires behave, studying how fires burn under various conditions. For example, wind, rain, and the dryness of the brush are all factors that affect how fires burn. Smokejumpers must be experts on

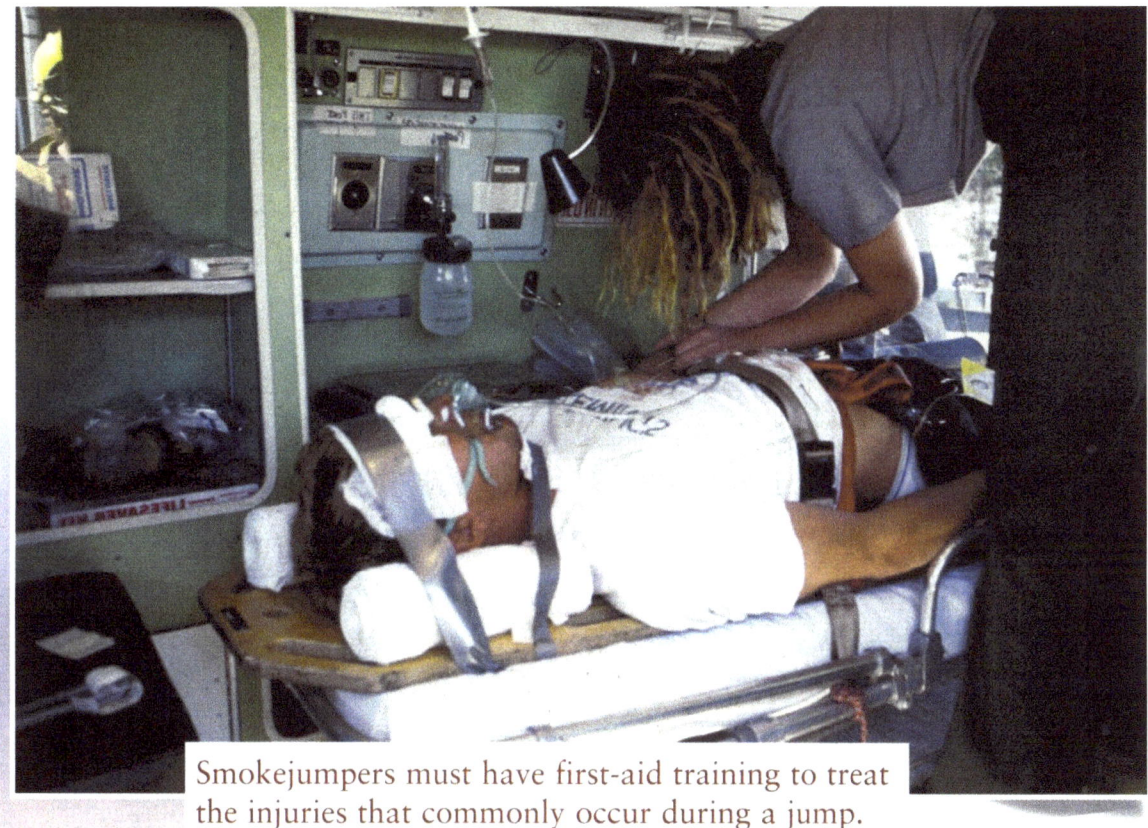

Smokejumpers must have first-aid training to treat the injuries that commonly occur during a jump.

fire since they drop from the sky into treacherous, fiery places. In order to fight fires properly, smokejumpers must know what to expect in a fire.

First Aid

Jumping from planes into dangerous areas can cause injuries. Sometimes, smokejumpers get away with only cuts and bruises on hard falls. Landing in a tree will certainly give a smokejumper a few scrapes and scratches. At other times, a fall onto rocky terrain can break an ankle or a leg. You probably think burns are common among smokejumpers, too. You're right. That's why every smokejumper must have first-aid training. Learning how to set your buddy's broken leg can save him or her a lot of pain while waiting for a chopper to come to the rescue. Smokejumpers use their first-aid skills often since it's not unusual for a smokejumper to get injured on the job.

Parachute Training

Smokejumping teachers are experienced smokejumpers themselves. They know the ins and outs of proper parachuting. At smokejumper school, these teachers use trampolines to show trainees how to properly hit the ground after a jump.

After trampoline training, trainees move on to tower training. Tower training takes place in a three-story tower. At a height of thirty feet in the air, trainees are hooked up to a wire that leads to the ground. A body harness suspends them from the wire as they slide at an angle down to the ground. Tower training teaches recruits what landing using a

During tower training, smokejumper recruits learn what it feels like to land with a parachute.

parachute feels like. No recruit jumps from or even steps into an airplane before successfully completing tower training.

Risk and Reward

Hard work and danger are a smokejumper's life. You might think that the Forest Service would have difficulty finding people who want to be smokejumpers. Yet each year, even though there are only about 150 smokejumper trainee positions open at the ten bases around the country, more than 700 people apply for those positions! The salary for a smokejumper is probably not the ultimate lure, although smokejumpers who work during the summer months make around $10,000 to $17,000, and year-round smokejumpers make between $40,000 and $60,000. However, between helping people and defending nature, you can probably see why being a smokejumper stirs up so many people's interest.

Jumping into a Fire

4

*E*very summer seems drier than the last up in the Rocky Mountains. Underbrush is like a tinderbox. A careless hiker or a flash of lightning could cause the area to quickly go up in flames. And then it happens. Lightning hits in a high gulch. Smoke is spotted from miles off. There are no roads nearby, and before long the wildfire may get out of control. This is a job for smokejumpers.

Danger lurks all around the smokejumpers. The airplane fights high winds caused by the rush of air from the blaze below. The plane must get the smokejumpers to the drop zone. There is no large clearing. Rocks line the mountainside. The area is remote. If the fire rages out of control, rescuing the smokejumpers will be difficult and dangerous. What is the plan?

Smokejumpers: Life Fighting Fires

Situations like this are almost a daily routine for smokejumpers. However, they trust that their training will help them overcome the obstacles that make fighting wildfires so difficult. Special uniforms, equipment, and tools also help smokejumpers fight wildfires as well as provide them with protection while they battle those blazes. Most of all, smokejumpers work together and help one another to make it through a long day—or days—of wildfire firefighting.

Jumpsuit and Safety Gear

You don't go to the beach without your swimsuit, do you? Of course not. Well, smokejumpers don't jump from an airplane into a firestorm without the right clothing, either. Smokejumpers wear lightweight jumpsuits made of fire-retardant material. The jumpsuits help keep them cool during the long workday digging a firebreak. Jumpsuits are either bright orange, white, or yellow. These colors can be easily seen from the air and through the trees. If a

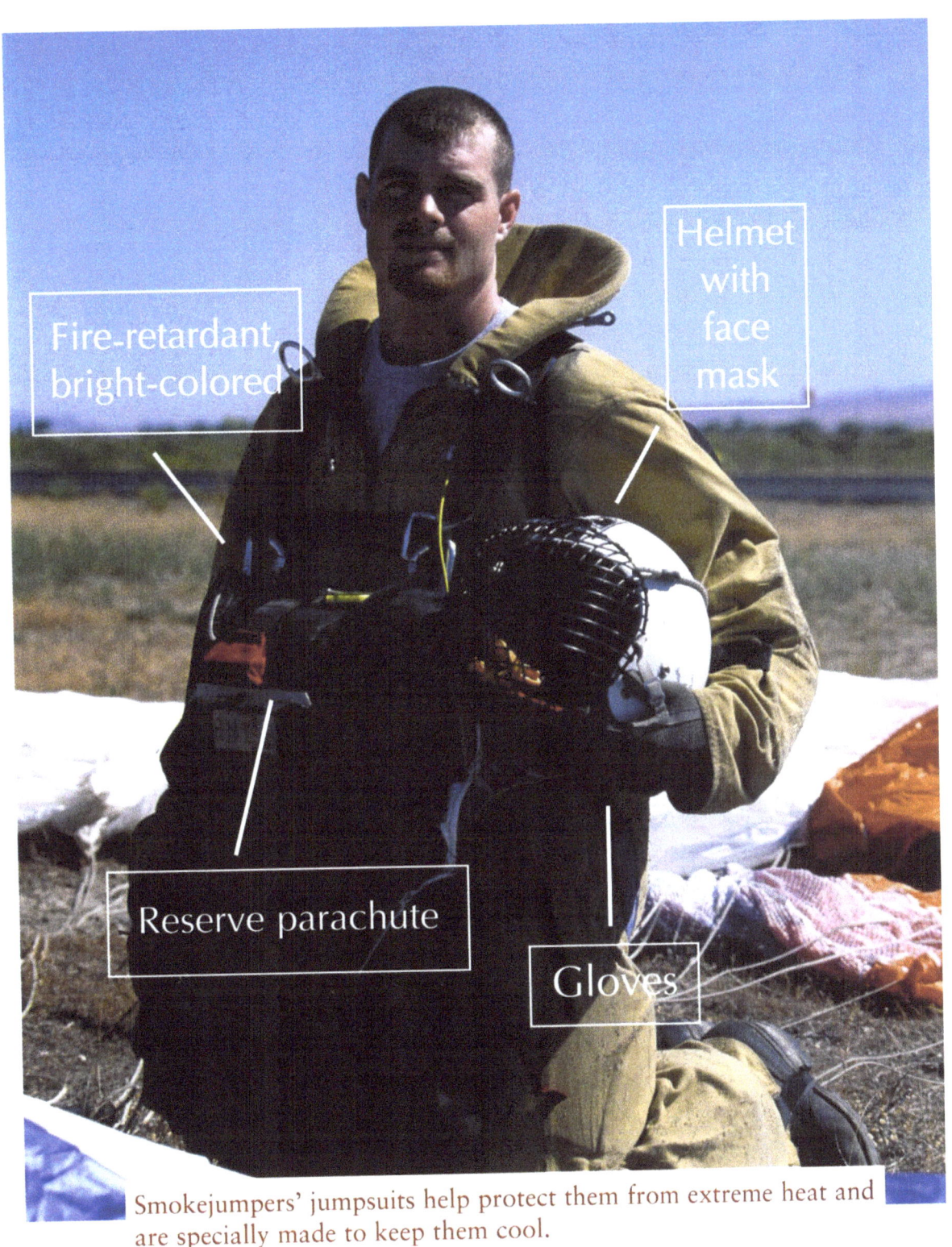

Smokejumpers' jumpsuits help protect them from extreme heat and are specially made to keep them cool.

Smokejumpers: Life Fighting Fires

smokejumper gets separated from his or her crew, or stick, during a jump or while fighting a blaze, a plane has a better chance of spotting the bright-colored suit.

Jumpsuits are padded to break the fall of a parachute jump. This is important in the rocky areas of a drop zone. Each jumpsuit has several large pockets for carrying small tools and the all-important safety line ladder. Smokejumpers also wear gloves while fighting wildfires. Gloves, however, are not worn during the jump because controlling a parachute is easier with bare hands.

A helmet and goggles are supplied to each smokejumper. The helmet is made of aluminum because this metal is lightweight and strong. Also, metal does not burn, so smokejumpers don't have to worry about burning embers floating around while they work. Attached to the helmet is a face mask, somewhat like the one on a football helmet. The face mask protects a smokejumper from branches when he or she lands in a tree. Goggles protect the eyes from wind, flying embers, branches, and smoke.

The Parachute

The master parachute rigger is in charge of packing each smokejumper's parachute. Parachutes must be packed in a certain way for them to unfold properly during a jump. A poorly packed parachute could tangle in its own ropes and send the smokejumper crashing to the ground.

As the plane carrying the smokejumpers nears the drop zone, the smokejumpers check their parachutes and gear. The parachute is attached to their backs by a harness. The harness is strapped around a jumper's shoulders, across the chest, and between the legs. The harness keeps the jumper attached to the parachute during the fall. An emergency parachute sits in a pack against the jumper's stomach.

The Jumpmaster

The jumpmaster does not jump with the smokejumpers. The jumpmaster's job is to make sure that the smokejumpers are jumping from the right place

The jumpmaster makes sure that smokejumpers are jumping from the right spot to land safely near a fire.

in the air so that they will land safely near the fire. The jumpmaster does this with the help of the airplane pilot. They both spot areas on the ground that could serve as the landing zone. Before the jumpmaster gives the signal to jump, however, he or she must be sure that the plane is in the right position. To do this, the jumpmaster drops crepe paper streamers out of the plane from 1,500 feet. This is the proper height for smokejumpers to jump from. The jumpmaster watches the streamers fall toward the

Jumping into a Fire

ground, and their path tells the jumpmaster if the wind direction is right for the smokejumpers to drop safely to the ground.

While the jumpmaster and the pilot spot for landing zones, the smokejumpers look out the window at the land below. They study the ground and the area near the fire. They need to know where clearings, rocky land, and the wildfire are located.

When the plane is positioned correctly, it circles the drop zone. The smokejumpers then prepare to

Smokejumpers hook their parachutes to a static line, which causes their chutes to open automatically when they jump.

Smokejumpers: Life Fighting Fires

Death by Fire

On August 5, 1949, a wildfire surrounded eighteen smokejumpers in Man Gulch, Montana. The Helena National Forest site became infamous because only three men survived—two smokejumpers and a foreman. The deaths shocked family and friends. These were the first deaths of smokejumpers since they had become part of the Forest Service nine years before.

jump. They hook their parachutes to a static line, which is a thick wire attached inside the plane that holds parachute release cords so that smokejumpers' chutes open automatically when they jump. When the chutes open, the smokejumpers don't just float down. Instead, they use the parachute "shroud lines" attached to the chute to steer toward the landing zone—and away from the fire. When the smokejumpers hit the ground, they roll to absorb the hard impact. They quickly pull their chutes onto the ground

Jumping into a Fire

and gather them to make sure no wind pulls the chutes and drags their bodies along the ground.

Sometimes smokejumpers may actually aim for trees if there is no clearing. Once caught on a tree, they drop themselves to the ground with their safety line. Smokejumpers get out of trees quickly. They don't want to be caught dangling from a branch when fire is nearby.

Bundled Tools

Once the smokejumpers have gathered themselves on the ground, they need their tools. The plane circles the area and drops more parachutes. These chutes hold packages containing tools, food supplies, or other equipment. If a stream, pond, or lake is near the fire, hoses and water pumps will be packed, too.

The parachutes are colored to identify what they are carrying. A red parachute's bundle might include shovels and saws. A yellow parachute might carry food supplies. Color-coded supply parachutes save

Smokejumpers: Life Fighting Fires

smokejumpers valuable time. The last thing a smokejumper needs is to find sandwiches when he or she is looking for a shovel!

Ready to Move Out

Once the supplies are gathered, the smokejumpers head toward the fire with all their gear on their backs. Now the real work begins. But before they can get to the fire's edge, the smokejumpers must determine where the fire is, where it might be heading, and the best way to tackle the blaze.

Fighting Forest Fires

5

Firefighters living in cities use water provided by fire hydrants to put out fires. High on a mountain, there are no fire hydrants. In fact, most of the time, there is little or no water. Smokejumpers must use what is around them. Since brush, pine needles, and timber burn, the only thing left with which to fight the fire is dirt.

Firebreaks

Without water to fight a fire, smokejumpers must make the fire burn itself out. The best way to do this is to take away the fire's fuel, which includes dry brush and grasses, fallen trees, and old logs. Making a firebreak does this job.

Smokejumpers: Life Fighting Fires

Smokejumpers choose an area away from the fire to make a firebreak. This chosen spot is directly in the path of the fire. Smokejumpers stay far away from the burning forest in order to make a firebreak. They must have time to cut down trees, dig up stumps, and drag away dry brush, since each of these is fuel for a fire. A strip of land that is cleared down to the dirt will not burn. Making a firebreak is a long, difficult job. Smokejumpers work against time as high winds and hot flames race toward them.

Even when the firebreak is completed, the smokejumpers' work is not done. The winds and flames working against them can still win. As a wildfire moves through a forest, it burns everything in its path. The cracking and popping you hear from a fireplace is a hundred times louder when it is coming from a wildfire. The burning and the heat send up hot, smoldering embers. The wind can carry these embers far through the air, often over the firebreak. If the embers land while they are still smoldering, they can easily start a new fire beyond the firebreak.

Smokejumpers must wait until the fire is completely out before they can claim victory. Therefore, they stand near the edge of the firebreak or back in the forest

A firebreak cannot always contain a fire. Smokejumpers stand by the edge of the firebreak and put out any new fires that flare up.

beyond the firebreak. They wait to see if new fires flare up. When some do—some always do—smokejumpers pounce on them with their shovels, turning dirt over onto the small flames until they are out.

At the edge of the firebreak that is creating a barrier against a dying wildfire, smokejumpers keep turning the soil. They need to make sure no smoldering logs, brush, or embers are able to survive. New fires have been known to break out three or four days later. Therefore, the soil is turned over and over.

Smokejumpers: Life Fighting Fires

Metal Safety Shelters

There have been times when fire has prevented smokejumpers from finding a safe path back to their team. For this deadly situation, the forest service has developed a fire shelter, a one-person tent made of a material coated with aluminum. The aluminum coating cannot burn and reflects heat. A smokejumper who is caught in a blaze can unfold the tent and curl up inside. The air trapped in the tent will keep the smokejumper alive while waiting to be rescued. Although the outside temperature may be 600 degrees, the inside of the safety shelter is no more than 130 degrees. Safety shelters have saved hundreds of lives.

Smokejumpers will even take off their gloves and feel the soil with their bare hands. They want to make sure it is not hot to the touch. Only then are they certain that the fire is dead.

Pulaskis, Chain Saws, and Elbow Grease

Wildfire firefighting is not incredibly high tech. Hot shot crews and smokejumpers use axes, chain saws, and muscle. These are the same tools that were used to fight wildfires almost one hundred years ago.

Fighting Forest Fires

Hot shot crews sometimes have bulldozers helping them build firebreaks. Bulldozers can be used when a wildfire is near a road, where they can be trucked in. Bulldozers easily knock over trees and plow over brush. Hot shot crews follow bulldozers along the firebreak, moving the trees, stumps, and brush across the firebreak. Smokejumpers don't have this luxury. They have only their muscles, stamina, and tools to fight fire.

The pulaski is the tool of choice, and a necessity, among hot shot crews and smokejumpers. The pulaski is a combination ax and hoe. Its edge is sharp to chop tree stumps, limbs, and brush, while its sides are curved to use for digging and turning the soil. This tool is named for Ed Pulaski, a park ranger who made the first one by hand in 1903. The pulaski has become so successful that today, the U.S. Forest Service purchases more than 35,000 new ones each year.

Chain saws also come in handy while

The pulaski, a combination of an ax and a hoe, is the tool of choice for smokejumpers.

Smokejumpers: Life Fighting Fires

building a firebreak. Their motor-driven cutting power quickly slices through thick trees and stumps. Every smokejumper uses a chain saw to bring down the biggest trees along a firebreak. Gas-powered cutting power is better than sawing by hand, which is how firefighters had to cut trees before the chain saw was invented.

Smokejumpers rely mostly on their bodies to fight fires. Their strength and stamina is what really powers the pulaskis and chain saws. It's the elbow grease that moves the trees, brush, and dirt. Fighting any fire is all about having the right tools to get the job done. That's why each fire is analyzed before smokejumpers are sent into a wildfire area. Dropping the correct number of smokejumpers into a fire also assures that the best possible effort is being made to fight the fire.

Smokejumpers work alone with a pulaski and chain saw. The veterans help the rookies work better and more efficiently. The rookies work harder than anyone to prove themselves worthy. The combined energy of ten or twenty—or even eighty—smokejumpers turns individual effort into a team victory against the blazing forest.

Fighting Forest Fires

Backfires

Sometimes the best way to make a fire burn itself out is to start another fire. Sounds crazy, doesn't it? It's not, but there are some risks.

Backfires are controlled fires that are set to burn a portion of forest so that the main wildfire has no more fuel. When a wildfire comes upon a backfire that has already burned up its fuel, the wildfire burns itself out.

Backfires are controlled fires that are set to burn a portion of a forest so that a larger wildfire has no more fuel.

Smokejumpers: Life Fighting Fires

Sometimes a backfire is started when there is not enough time to build a firebreak. Maybe the blaze is out of control and it would be too dangerous to send in smokejumpers. Maybe there aren't enough smokejumpers to send into an area and successfully fight the blaze before it gets out of control or threatens the smokejumpers' lives. Other times a backfire is started after a firebreak has already been built. Maybe the wildfire is moving too quickly and it can easily jump an existing firebreak. Whatever the situation, the decision to start a backfire is difficult. If a backfire is started and the wind shifts, that fire can easily burn even more forest. Then there will be two fires! Starting a backfire is a calculated risk, but it is often the best choice for the most dangerous situations.

Once a backfire is started, smokejumpers stick around and make sure the fires burn themselves out. They dig in the ground and cover smoldering embers with dirt. They turn the soil and stamp out small fires. Smokejumpers treat a backfire like any other fire.

Fighting Forest Fires

Help from the Skies

Sometimes smokejumpers do get high-tech help fighting fires. When fires burn out of control, almost nothing can stop their destructive paths. The few high-tech weapons available today come from the sky.

Air Tankers

Airplanes and helicopters are now put to use fighting fires. Specially made tanks have been installed

Flame retardant is used to fight wildfires from the air.

Smokejumpers: Life Fighting Fires

in airplanes to hold water or flame retardant. The planes fly low over the fire and drop their loads atop the flames. Helicopters work almost the same way. They carry huge buckets suspended from cables. When using water, they lower the buckets into a lake near the wildfire. The buckets settle in the lake and fill with water. Then the helicopters pull the full buckets from the lake and fly over the fire to dump their loads.

For almost thirty years, flame retardant has been used to fight wildfires from the air. Since water evaporates quickly, unless it is dropped right on top of the fire, it usually does little good. Retardant is a chemical that does not evaporate. It is a soupy liquid that is thicker than water. It is also sticky. When the retardant is dropped over an area, it sticks to leaves, trees, and the ground. As the wildfire approaches an area spread with retardant, the retardant slows the fire's progress. This allows smokejumpers and other ground crews time to build firebreaks. Retardant is colored so that a plane knows where it has already dumped it. This way, the retardant is not wasted.

Fighting Forest Fires

Living in an Oven

Raging wildfires happen during the summer, so it's already hot. Add to that the task of actually fighting a fire for several days and you feel like you're being slow-roasted in an oven. There is little a smokejumper can do but concentrate on his or her job during this time. No luxuries exist in a remote part of a forest. You are either working or you are eating and resting

Life as a smokejumper is not luxurious. Military-style rations of canned goods are standard fare.

Smokejumpers: Life Fighting Fires

in order to work some more. When a fire is too large to put out in a single day, smokejumpers must stay overnight. Sometimes smokejumpers are in the field for several days.

When fires last more than a day, airplanes return to drop more food rations. Smokejumpers live on sandwiches and canned goods. The canned goods are much like military-style food. At the end of a long day working against a fire, smokejumpers must gather supply canisters and find a safe area to sleep in for the night.

Getting Home Safely

Putting out a wildfire may be the job that smokejumpers are sent to do, but the first order of business is to keep everyone safe. Over the many years smokejumpers have been fighting wildfires, very few of them have died. This is because safety precautions are taken before, during, and after a fire is fought. As crazy as these men and women who work as smokejumpers may seem, they have no death wish. The opposite is true. They love the environment and want

Fighting Forest Fires

to help keep it safe for animals and humans. Their job is extremely dangerous, but they are professionals. They understand the risks, and know what to do to avoid death.

When the fire has been smothered and all the work is done, it's time for the smokejumpers to return to base. But since they dropped from the skies into this remote area, how will they get out? Often by the same method they got in. The team radios its base and calls for a helicopter to come pick the smokejumpers up. Sometimes the team must walk a long way to get to a clearing where a helicopter can land. This walk is a victory march. The success the team has achieved by putting out a destructive fire is well worth the few hours that smokejumpers must hike to get to a rescue area. When all are aboard, a cheer goes up. They're going home.

Glossary

azimuth indicator Scientific instrument used to convert direction into a numerical compass reading.

backfire Fire set to burn a section of forest up to the wildfire so that the two fires will burn each other out.

endurance A person's ability to work a long time without giving in to fatigue.

firebreak Long, wide dirt clearing used to stop a wildfire.

Fire Scan Type of photography that uses infrared film to see through smoke and clouds.

gulch Small, deep valley.

habitat Where something lives.

hot shots Nickname for ground-crew teams of wildfire firefighters.

Glossary

ignite To start a fire.

jumpmaster Person who spots the best place on the ground for smokejumpers to land.

ladder Safety line used by smokejumpers to lower themselves from the trees in which they get caught during parachute drops.

lookout towers Ninety-foot-tall towers with cabins to house firewatcher lookouts.

master parachute rigger Person who properly packs all smokejumper parachutes.

packout test Smokejumper test that has a recruit carry a 110-pound equipment pack over a three-mile course in less than ninety minutes.

pulaski Tool used in wildfire firefighting that is half-ax, half-hoe.

static line Thick wire attached inside a plane that holds parachute release cords so that a parachute opens when a smokejumper jumps out of the plane.

sticks Nickname for smokejumper teams.

topsoil First two to three feet of soil that covers land.

watersheds Underground channels that supply rivers and streams with rainwater.

wildfire Fire burning in a forest.

For More Information

International Association of Wildland Fire
4025 FairRidge Drive
Fairfax, VA 22033-2868
(703)273-9815 ext.314
Web site: http://www.iawfonline.org

International Firefighters and Police Officers Association
23672 San Vincent Road
Suite 364
Ramona, CA 92065-4245
(760) 789-4391
Web site: http://www.ramonamall.com/ifpa.html
e-mail: ifpa@flash.net

For More Information

National Fire Protection Association (NFPA)
1 Batterymarch Park
P.O. Box 9101
Quincy, MA 02269-9101
(617) 770-3000
Web site: http://www.nfpa.org

National Interagency Fire Center (NIFC)
3833 South Development Avenue
Boise, Idaho 83705-5354
(208) 387-5512
Web site: http://www.nifc.gov

National Smokejumper Association
P.O. Box 4081
Missoula, MT 49806
(406) 549-9938
Web site: http://www.smokejumpers.com

Wildfire Training Network
Web site: http://www.wildfiretrainingnet.com

Smokejumpers: Life Fighting Fires
In Canada

Canadian Forests
4660 Brentlawn Drive
Burnaby, BC V5C 3V2
(604) 299-9643
Web site: http://www.canadian-forests.com
e-mail: roper@canadian-forests.com

Canadian Interagency Forest Fire Centre
210-301 Weston Street
Winnipeg, MB R3E 3H4
(204) 784-2030
Website: http://www.ciffc.ca

Web Sites

Due to the changing nature of Internet links, the Rosen Publishing Group, Inc., has developed an online list of Web sites related to the subject of this book. This site is updated regularly. Please use this link to access the list:

http://www.rosenlinks.com/ec/smju

For Further Reading

Ermitage, Kathleen. *Firefighter*. Chatham, NJ: Raintree Steck-Vaughn Publishers, 2000.

Fortney, Mary T. *Fire Station Number 4: The Daily Life of Firefighters*. Minneapolis, MN: Carolrhoda Books, 1998.

Greenberg, Keith Elliot. *Smokejumper: Firefighter from the Sky*. Woodbridge, CT: Blackbirch Press, 1995.

Maze, Stephanie. *I Want to Be a Firefighter*. San Diego, CA: Harcourt Brace and Company, 1999.

Taylor, Murry A. *Jumping Fire: A Smokejumper's Memoir of Fighting Wildfires*. San Diego, CA: Harcourt Brace and Company, 2000.

Index

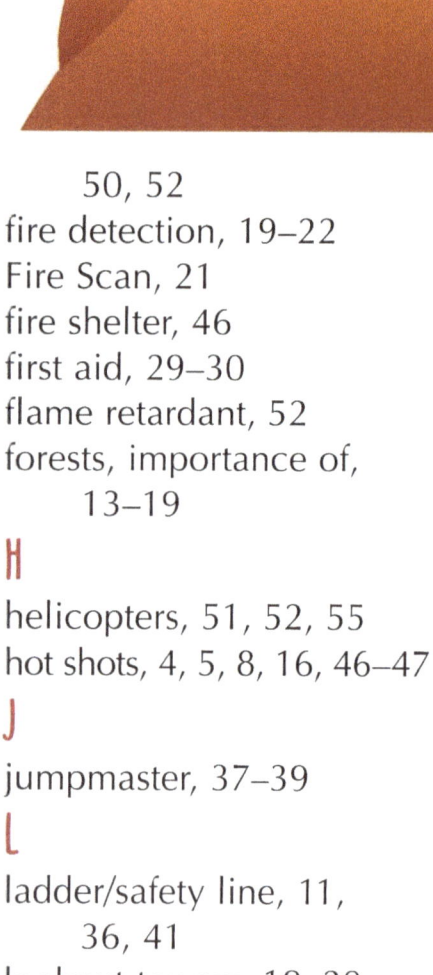

A
airplanes, 4, 8, 11, 19, 21, 29, 32, 33, 36, 37, 38, 51–52, 54
animals, in forests, 5, 13–15, 55
axes, 46, 47

B
backfires, 49–50
bulldozers, 47

C
chain saws, 46, 48

D
drop/landing zones, 8, 10–11, 33, 36, 37, 38, 39, 40

F
firebreak, 6, 43–46, 47, 48, 50, 52
fire detection, 19–22
Fire Scan, 21
fire shelter, 46
first aid, 29–30
flame retardant, 52
forests, importance of, 13–19

H
helicopters, 51, 52, 55
hot shots, 4, 5, 8, 16, 46–47

J
jumpmaster, 37–39

L
ladder/safety line, 11, 36, 41
lookout towers, 19–20

Index

M
master parachute
- rigger, 37
- training, 30–32

P
parachuting, 4, 7, 8, 9, 11, 23, 24, 26, 36, 37–41
pulaski, 47, 48

R
root systems, importance of, 16–18

S
smoke, 20, 21, 33, 36
smokejumpers/smoke-jumping,
- duties of, 5–6, 24, 42, 43–46, 47, 48, 50
- equipment and safety gear, 34–42, 46–48
- hazards of, 11, 12, 26, 29–30, 36, 40, 41, 46
- history of, 7–9
- requirements for, 9, 11, 23, 24, 25–28, 47, 48
- salary, 32
- training for, 23–32, 34, 48
- working conditions, 24, 53–54

spotter, 11, 22
spotter planes, 19, 21
stick crews, 9, 10, 36

U
U.S. Forest Service, 8, 9, 21, 32, 47

W
weather forecasting, 21–22
weather satellites, 19, 22
wildfires,
- dangers/threats of, 5, 11, 12, 13, 15, 33–34, 36, 41, 44, 50
- how they start, 10, 22, 33
- stopping, 5–6, 8, 43–46, 49–50, 51–52
- tracking/spotting, 5, 19–20, 21, 38, 42, 48

wood products, 15–16

Smokejumpers: Life Fighting Fires

About the Author

Mark Beyer was born in Chicago and has traveled throughout the world. He earned an MFA from Columbia College-Chicago in 1998. He now lives and writes in New Port Richey, Florida.

Photo Credits

Cover © 2000 Dave Bentz; p. 5 © Darrell Gulin/Corbis; pp. 7, 51 © Archive Photo; pp. 6, 21, 29, 31, 35, 38, 39, 45, 47, 49, 53 © Mike McMillan; pp. 9, 18 © Corbis; p. 14 © U.S. Fish & Wildlife Service; p. 17 © David Muench/Corbis; pp. 20, 22, 24–25, 27 © AP Photo Worldwide; p. 26 courtesy of Deanne Shulman.

Design and Layout

Les Kanturek

www.ingramcontent.com/pod-product-compliance
Lightning Source LLC
Chambersburg PA
CBHW041114070526
44584CB00002B/170